My First Picture
Encyclopedia

Show Me
DINOSAURS

by Janet Riehecky

raintree

a Capstone company — publishers for children

Raintree is an imprint of Capstone Global Library Limited, a company incorporated in England and Wales having its registered office at 264 Banbury Road, Oxford, OX2 7DY – Registered company number: 6695582

www.raintree.co.uk
myorders@raintree.co.uk

Aaron Sautter, editor; Heidi Thompson, designer; Svetlana Zhurkin, media researcher; Laura Manthe, production specialist
Printed and bound in China.

ISBN 978 1 474 73346 5
21 20 19 18 17
10 9 8 7 6 5 4 3 2 1

British Library Cataloguing in Publication Data
A full catalogue record for this book is available from the British Library.

Acknowledgements
We would like to thank the following for permission to reproduce photographs: Corbis: Stocktrek Images/Walter Myers, 6 (left); Corel, cover (bottom right), 11 (top left), 12 (bottom right), 13 (all), 14 (middle and bottom), 15 (top left), 16, 17 (top and bottom), 18, 19 (top and middle left), 20 (right), 21 (middle), 24 (top); Dreamstime: Andrey Troitskiy, 12 (top), Elena Duvernay, 11 (bottom left), Zoran Stojkovic, 26 (top); Getty Images: UIG/Encyclopaedia Britannica, 19 (bottom); iStockphotos: bortonia (maps), 6, 7, Josh Laverty, 14 (top), Quan Long, 9 (bottom right); Library of Congress, 31 (middle and bottom); National Geographic Stock: Lowell Georgia, 30 (top); Newscom: AFP Photo/Mark Klingler/Carnegie Museum of Natural History, 9 (top), AFP/Portia Sloan, 22 (top right), Custom Medical Stock Photo/L. Birmingham, 17 (middle right), Florilegius/Album, 29 (bottom), Getty Images/AFP/Chuang Zhao and Lida Xing, 21 (bottom), Photoshot/World Pictures/Rick Strange, 27 (top), ZUMA Press, 21 (top); Photo Researchers: David Parker, 28 (bottom), Laurie O'Keefe, 27 (bottom); Shutterstock: Catmando, 5 (middle), 17 (middle left), dezignor, 28 (top), DM7, cover (top right), 1 (top right), Dr_Flash, 29 (top), Eric Isselée, 5 (top), Esteban De Armas, 7 (bottom), ExpressionImage, 24 (bottom), Iwona Grodzka (torn paper), cover, 1, Jean-Michel Girard, back cover (middle right and left), 12 (bottom left), 25 (top right), Jiang Hongyan, back cover (top), 8 (top left), Kostyantyn Salanda, 10, Linda Bucklin, cover (bottom left), 4 (left), 5 (bottom), 6 (right), 11 (bottom right), 19 (middle right), 25 (middle), Madlen, back cover (bottom), 8 (bottom left), Michael Rosskothen, 15 (top right and bottom right), 22 (bottom), 23 (top), 25 (top left), Praisaeng, 9 (middle), Preto Perola, 26 (bottom), Ralf Juergen Kraft, 4 (right), Sofia Santos, cover (back and bottom middle), back cover (back), 1 (back), 2, 23 (bottom right), Steffen Foerster Photography, 30 (bottom), Steve Collender, 8 (right), thinkdo, 31 (top), Vasily Vishnevskiy, 9 (bottom left); Wikipedia, 11 (top right), Ballista, 23 (bottom left), Franko Fonseca, 25 (bottom), Ghedoghedo, 22 (top left), Nobu Tamura, 20 (left), Public Library of Science, 15 (bottom right)

We would like to thank Mathew J. Wedel for his invaluable help in the preparation of this book.

Every effort has been made to contact copyright holders of material reproduced in this book. Any omissions will be rectified in subsequent printings if notice is given to the publisher.

All the Internet addresses (URLs) given in this book were valid at the time of going to press. However, due to the dynamic nature of the Internet, some addresses may have changed, or sites may have changed or ceased to exist since publication. While the author and publisher regret any inconvenience this may cause readers, no responsibility for any such changes can be accepted by either the author or the publisher.

The author dedicates this book to her husband, John, and thanks him for his loving support.

Contents

What is a dinosaur?

Dinosaur means 'terrible lizard'. These amazing creatures ruled Earth for about 160 million years. How do scientists recognize these ancient reptiles?

It's in the bones

Special features tell scientists whether a bone belongs to a dinosaur or some other animal. All dinosaurs had a hole in their hip bones that allowed their legs to stand straight under their bodies.

bird-hipped

hip bones that point backwards; all plant eaters except long-necked dinosaurs had bird hips

lizard-hipped

hip bones that point forwards; big meat eaters and long-necked plant eaters had lizard hips

cold-blooded

when an animal's body temperature is the same as its surroundings; reptiles like turtles and lizards are cold-blooded

warm-blooded

when an animal's body temperature stays about the same all the time; dinosaurs were probably warm-blooded

Were they dinosaurs?

Dinosaurs were land animals. Many flying and swimming reptiles like pteranodon (teh-RAN-uh-don) and plesiosaurus (PLEE-see-uh-sore-us) lived alongside the dinosaurs. But they are not considered true dinosaurs.

When did the dinosaurs live?

Scientists think Earth is about 4.5 billion years old. Dinosaurs lived between 230 million and 65 million years ago before they became extinct.

extinct

no longer living; an extinct animal is one that has died out, with no more of its kind

Mesozoic Era

(mez-uh-ZOH-ik) span of time from 251 million years ago to 65.5 million years ago; it is best known as the Age of Dinosaurs

Triassic Period

(try-AS-sik) dates from 251 million years ago to 199 million years ago; dinosaurs first appeared on Earth about halfway through this period

Jurassic Period

(joo-RAS-ik) dates from 199 million years ago to 145 million years ago; this was the time of giant dinosaurs

Pangea

At the beginning of the Triassic Period, all of the land on Earth was part of one big continent called Pangea (pan-JEE-uh). By the end of the Cretaceous Period, the land had split into pieces similar to the present continents.

Present Day

Cretaceous Period

(kri-TEY-shuhs) dates from 145 million years ago to 65 million years ago; dinosaurs disappeared at the end of this period

mass extinction

when many types of plants and animals become extinct at the same time; about 75 per cent of all living creatures on Earth, including most dinosaurs, became extinct at the end of the Mesozoic Era

What was the dinosaurs' world like?

Earth's land and climate were very different during the time of the dinosaurs. Early in the Mesozoic Era, there were many deserts. As the climate became warmer and wetter, large forests began to cover most of the land. Flowering plants and new kinds of animals began to appear in the Cretaceous Period.

ginkgo

a tree with fan-shaped leaves; ginkgo trees were common in the Mesozoic Era

conifers

trees that grow needles instead of leaves; conifers were the biggest trees during the time of the dinosaurs

cycads

plants that look like ferns or palm trees; cycad trees were common in the Jurassic Period

mammals

warm-blooded animals that have backbones and hair or fur; female mammals feed milk to their young; most mammals that lived with the dinosaurs were small, shrewlike creatures

climate

the weather conditions over a period of time

reptiles

cold-blooded animals with backbones; dry scales cover a reptile's body; reptiles like turtles, lizards and crocodiles lived alongside the dinosaurs

birds

warm-blooded animals that have feathers and wings and lay eggs; birds have legs directly under their bodies like dinosaurs; most scientists believe birds are living dinosaurs

insects

small animals with a hard outer shell, six legs, three body sections and two antennae; flies, ants, mosquitoes, cockroaches and many other insects lived with the dinosaurs

Long-necked dinosaurs

The biggest dinosaurs that ever lived were huge plant eaters. These giants travelled in herds across the countryside. Most ate hundreds of kilograms of food every day. Their huge size protected them from most predators.

brachiosaurus

(BRAK-ee-uh-sore-us) weighed as much as six elephants; its front legs were longer than its back legs, like a giraffe

How brontosaurus lost its name

In 1879 scientists found a skeleton that they named brontosaurus (bron-tuh-SORE-uhs). They later realized it was the same as the apatosaurus that was found in 1877. Since it was named apatosaurus first, that's the name scientists use today.

predator

an animal that hunts other animals for food

apatosaurus

(ah-PAT-uh-sore-us) first discovered in 1877, scientists at first gave it the head from a different dinosaur by mistake; the correct head was identified 100 years later

mamenchisaurus

(mah-MEN-chee-sore-us) almost half its length came from its neck, which was 11 m (36 feet) long

argentinosaurus

(ahr-gen-TEEN-uh-sore-us) might have been the heaviest dinosaur that ever lived; it weighed between 54 and 64 metric tons (60 and 70 tons)

sauroposeidon

(sore-uh-poh-SEYE-don) may have been the tallest of all dinosaurs; it stood up to 18 m (60 feet) tall

Duck-billed dinosaurs

These plant-eaters usually grazed on all four feet. But they could run on two feet with their stiff tails stretched out for balance.

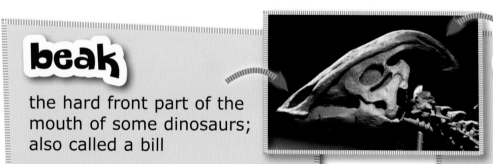

beak

the hard front part of the mouth of some dinosaurs; also called a bill

crest

a bony ridge on the heads of some dinosaurs; crests may have helped dinosaurs recognize each other, attract a mate or make sounds

parasaurolophus

(PAIR-a-sore-o-lo-fus)
a long, hollow crest extended behind its head

edmontosaurus

(ed-MON-tuh-sore-us)
it ate conifer needles, twigs, seeds and fruits; scientists have learned a lot from two mummified bodies of this dinosaur

corythosaurus

(ko-RITH-uh-sore-us) had a hollow crest shaped like a half moon

lambeosaurus

(LAM-bee-uh-sore-us) a hatchet-shaped crest slanted forwards on its head; its young had shorter, more rounded crests

hadrosaurus

(HAY-druh-sore-us) first dinosaur found in North America; it was discovered in 1858 and is the official state dinosaur of New Jersey

shantungosaurus

(shan-TUNG-uh-sore-us) may have been the largest duck-billed dinosaur; it grew 15 m (50 feet) long and weighed 14 metric tons (15 tons)

Horned dinosaurs

These spiky plant-eating dinosaurs had thick bodies, short tails and parrot-like beaks. They walked on four legs and lived in herds. Many had horns and frills.

frill

a bony collar that fanned out from the back of a dinosaur's skull; frills came in many sizes and shapes

horn

a hard, bony growth on the heads of some dinosaurs; horns were usually pointed and may have been used for self-defence

triceratops

(try-SAYR-uh-tops) had two long horns on its forehead and a shorter horn on its nose; triceratops was one of the last dinosaurs to become extinct

centrosaurus

(SEN-truh-sore-us) had one horn on its nose; this dinosaur was probably big enough to protect itself from predators

styracosaurus

(sty-RACK-uh-sore-us) had several long horns and spikes on the top and sides of its frill; it also had a long horn on its nose

pentaceratops

(pent-uh-SAYR-uh-tops) had a frill with two large holes that were covered with skin; its name means 'five-horned face', but it had only three horns

kosmoceratops

(KOZZ-mo-sayr-uh-tops) had 13 horns on its frill and two spikes sticking out from its cheeks; its horns all curved down and may have been used to attract a mate

diabloceratops

(dee-AB-low-sayr-uh-tops) had two horns on its forehead and two large horns on its frill; its name means 'devil-horned faced'

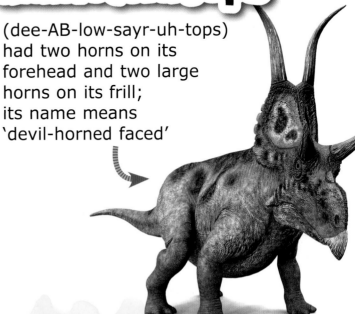

Armoured and plated dinosaurs

These plant-eating dinosaurs had short legs, thick bodies and small heads. Their armoured bodies were often covered with thick, bony scutes. Some had bony spikes or plates on their backs and tails.

stegosaurus

(STEG-uh-sore-uhs) a double row of plates on its back may have been used as defence against predators; it also had four spikes on the end of its tail

scute

horny or bony plate that grows on the skin

euoplocephalosaurus

(you-oh-plo-SEFF-uh-luh-sore-uhs) armour and spikes were almost everywhere on its body, even on its eyelids; it also carried a bony club on the end of its tail

nodosaurus

(NO-doe-sore-uhs) covered with bony scutes; it may have also had long spikes on its shoulders or sides

ankylosaurus

(ang-KIL-uh-sore-uhs)–built like a tank, its thick armour was formed from scutes; it had a large bony club on the end of its tail for self-defence

sauropelta

(sore-uh-PELT-uh) had six short spikes on its neck and two large spikes on its shoulders

Ostrich dinosaurs

These dinosaurs looked similar to ostriches of today. They had short bodies, long necks and small heads with large eyes. They also had short arms and long tails. These fast-running dinosaurs usually lived in herds.

gizzard stones

rocks that some dinosaurs swallowed with their food; the rocks went into a sack called a gizzard where they broke food into small pieces to be digested; scientists think ostrich dinosaurs ate plants, insects and some small animals

gallimimus

(gal-ih-MIME-uhs) one of the biggest ostrich dinosaurs; it grew up to 3.4 m (11 feet) tall and weighed up to 454 kg (1,000 pounds)

struthiomimus

(stroo-thee-uh-MIME-uhs) had very large eyes on either side of its head; it had excellent vision to see everything around it

dromiceiomimus

(dro-mih-SAY-uh-mime-uhs) possibly the fastest of all ostrich dinosaurs; it could run as fast as 80 km (50 miles) per hour

pelicanimimus

(PEL-uh-can-uh-mime-uhs) one of the earliest known ostrich dinosaurs; it had as many as 220 small teeth and a pouch similar to a pelican's

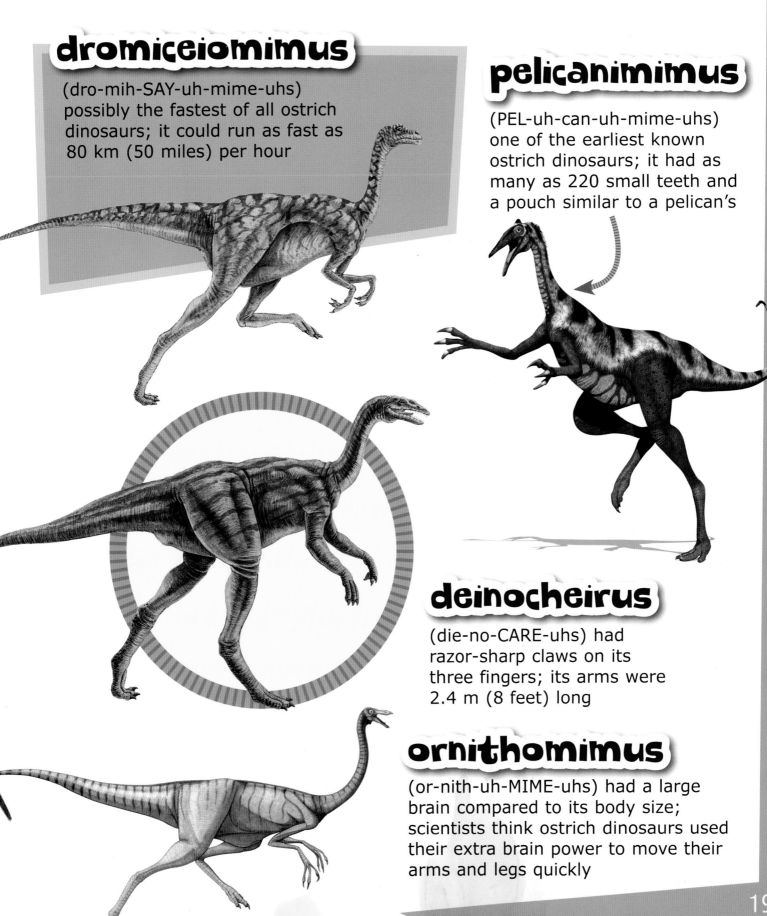

deinocheirus

(die-no-CARE-uhs) had razor-sharp claws on its three fingers; its arms were 2.4 m (8 feet) long

ornithomimus

(or-nith-uh-MIME-uhs) had a large brain compared to its body size; scientists think ostrich dinosaurs used their extra brain power to move their arms and legs quickly

Small meat eaters

Most small meat-eating dinosaurs walked on two legs. They kept their long tails stretched out behind them for balance. They usually hunted in packs and used sharp teeth and claws to catch and eat small prey.

scavenger

an animal that feeds on animals that are already dead; some small meat eaters probably ate the remains of animals killed by bigger predators

coelophysis

(see-low-FYE-sis) had a long neck and a lightweight body; its beak-like mouth was similar to a bird's; thousands of coelophysis bones have been found at Ghost Ranch quarry in New Mexico, USA

compsognathus

(comp-sog-NATH-us) about the size of a chicken; it grabbed and held prey with its three-fingered hands

prey

an animal that is hunted by other animals for food

ornitholestes

(or-nith-oh-LEST-eez) this little predator used its powerful jaws to quickly snatch and kill its prey; it may have raided the nests of early birds to look for food

anchiornis

(ANN-chee-or-niss) the smallest dinosaur ever found; it was only 30 cm (1 foot) tall and weighed about 113 g (4 ounces); its body was covered in feathers and it had short wings, but it could not fly

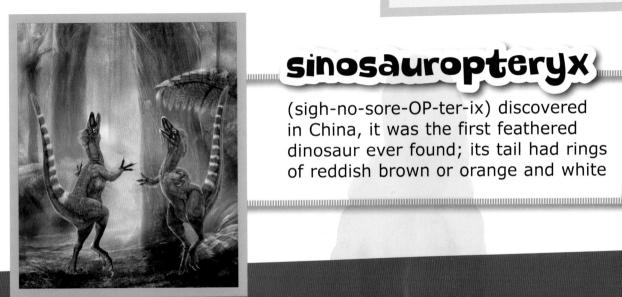

sinosauropteryx

(sigh-no-sore-OP-ter-ix) discovered in China, it was the first feathered dinosaur ever found; its tail had rings of reddish brown or orange and white

Raptors

Raptors had slender bodies and walked on two legs. Most raptors had a large, sickle-shaped claw on each foot. Many were covered in feathers.

microraptor

(MY-kro-rap-tohr) had two wings on its arms and two more on its legs; scientists think it could glide through the air

sickle-shaped claw

a sharp, curved claw used for slashing at prey; raptors usually carried these claws upright to keep them from dragging on the ground

velociraptor

(veh-LOSS-i-rap-tohr) it could run up to 64 km (40 miles) per hour in short bursts; it hunted in packs

deinonychus

(die-nuh-NYE-kuss)
about 1.5 m (5 feet) tall, it hunted in packs to take down large prey; its name means 'terrible claw'

utahraptor

(YOU-tah-rap-tohr) may be the largest of all raptors; it grew up to 7 m (23 feet) long and had a sickle claw almost 30 cm (1 foot) long

bambiraptor

(BAM-bee-rap-tohr)
about the size of a chicken; it was first discovered in Montana, USA by 14-year-old Wes Linster

Large meat eaters

These huge predators had large heads and powerful jaws filled with sharp serrated teeth. Their feet were tipped with huge, powerful claws. Most giant meat eaters probably lived alone or with a small family.

serrated

saw-toothed

megalosaurus

(MEG-a-loh-sore-uhs) the first dinosaur to be given a scientific name; its name means 'great lizard'

tyrannosaurus

(ty-RAN-uh-sore-uhs) scientists think it could eat up to 227 kg (500 pounds) of meat in one bite; its name means 'tyrant lizard'

spinosaurus

(SPINE-uh-sore-uhs) the largest of all known meat-eating dinosaurs; it grew up to 6 m (20 feet) tall and weighed up to 8 metric tons (9 tons); it had a large sail on its back

allosaurus

(AL-uh-sore-uhs) the top predator of the late Jurassic Period; it had two bony ridges on its head and a pair of horns above its eyes

giganotosaurus

(gig-uh-NOTE-uh-sore-uhs)– had the biggest skull of any known meat-eating dinosaur; it looked similar to tyrannosaurus

carcharodontosaurus

(car-kah-roe-DON-toh-sore-uhs) had a large head and a small brain; its name means 'shark-toothed lizard'

Dinosaur life cycle

Dinosaurs all began life in an egg. But after they hatched, most young dinosaurs grew quickly.

egg

a round object with a shell in which young animals develop; the biggest dinosaur eggs ever found were about the size of a football

nest

a hole that dinosaurs dug into sand or dirt to lay their eggs; dinosaur nests could be up to 1.8 m (6 feet) wide

Keeping eggs warm

Most dinosaurs were too big and heavy to sit on their eggs. They may have covered their eggs with plants to keep them warm instead. Plants produce heat as they decay.

decay

to break down or rot

hatchlings

a young animal that has just come out of its egg; some dinosaur hatchlings could care for themselves as soon as they hatched

young

the offspring of an animal; young dinosaurs were often protected by older dinosaurs in herds

Growing up

Like most animals today, dinosaurs learned to hunt and defend themselves by watching their elders. They practised these skills as they played.

mate

to join together to produce young; many dinosaurs probably had brightly colored crests or frills to help attract a mate

Caring mothers

Many dinosaurs simply laid their eggs and left. But some dinosaur mothers cared for their babies. Fossils in Montana, USA showed young maiasaura (MY-uh-sore-uh) still living in nests. Their mothers must have brought them food and protected them. Maiasaura means 'good mother lizard'.

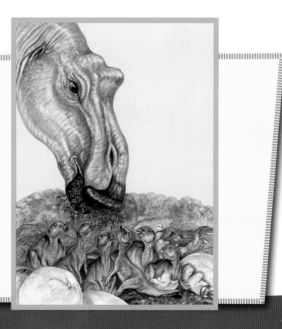

How did dinosaurs go extinct?

Most scientists think that a huge asteroid hit Earth 65 million years ago. They believe it caused the extinction of the dinosaurs. The 9.7-km (6-mile) wide asteroid hit Earth at the Yucatán peninsula in Mexico.

asteroid

a large space rock that moves around the sun

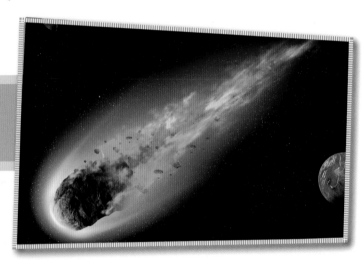

Melted rocks

Scientists have found rocks that were exposed to intense heat 65 million years ago. These rocks support the idea of a large asteroid hitting Earth.